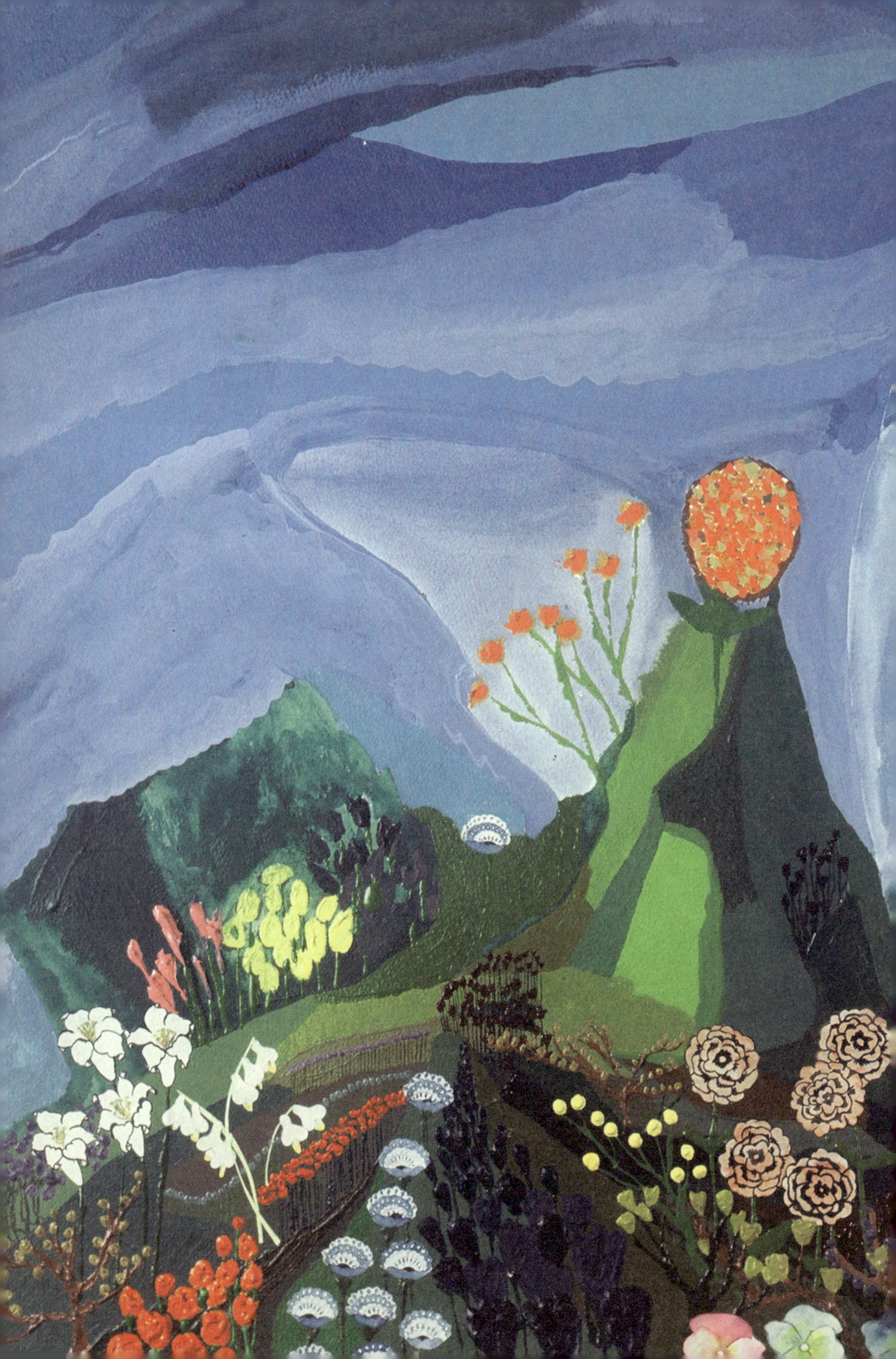

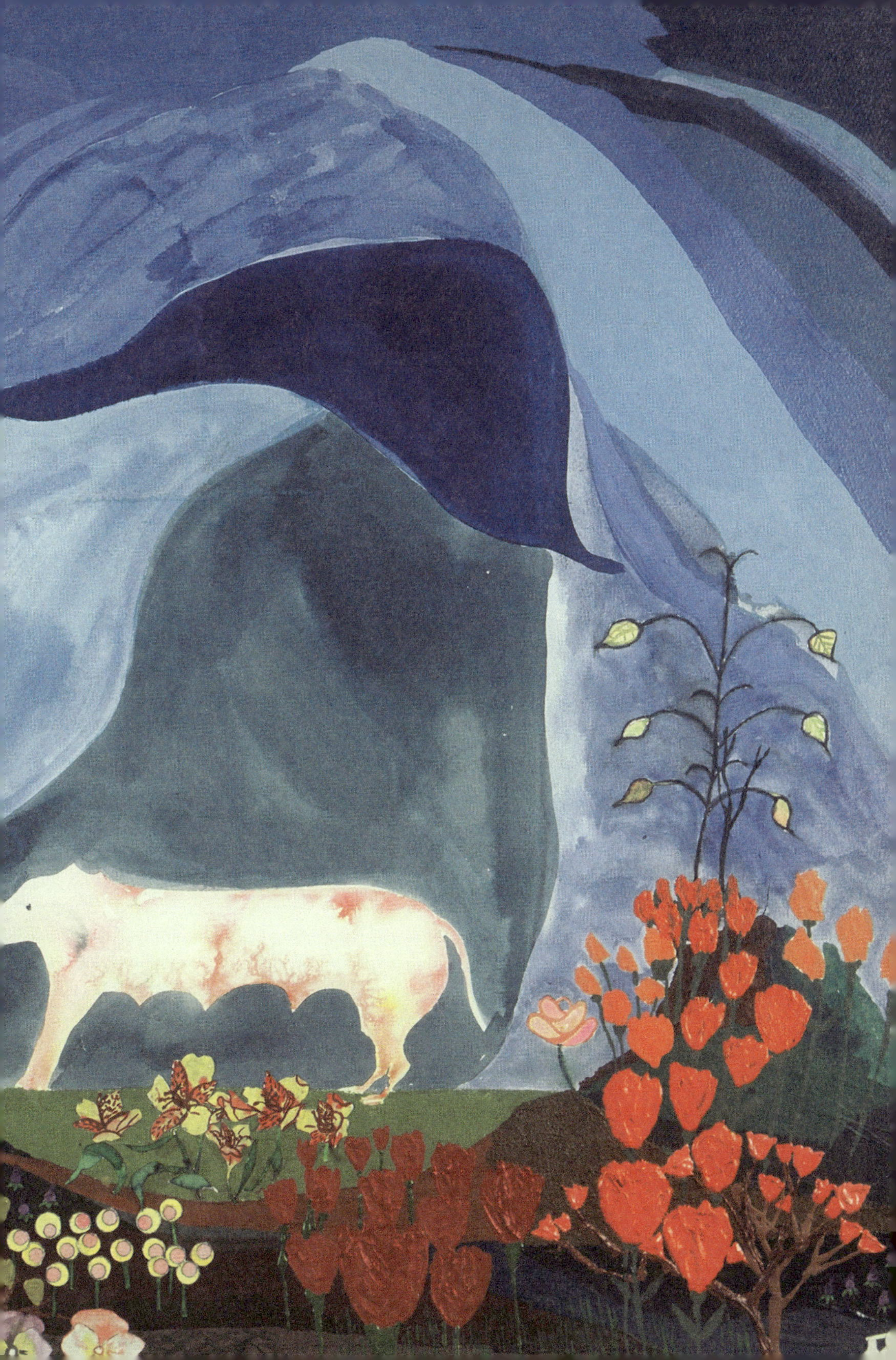

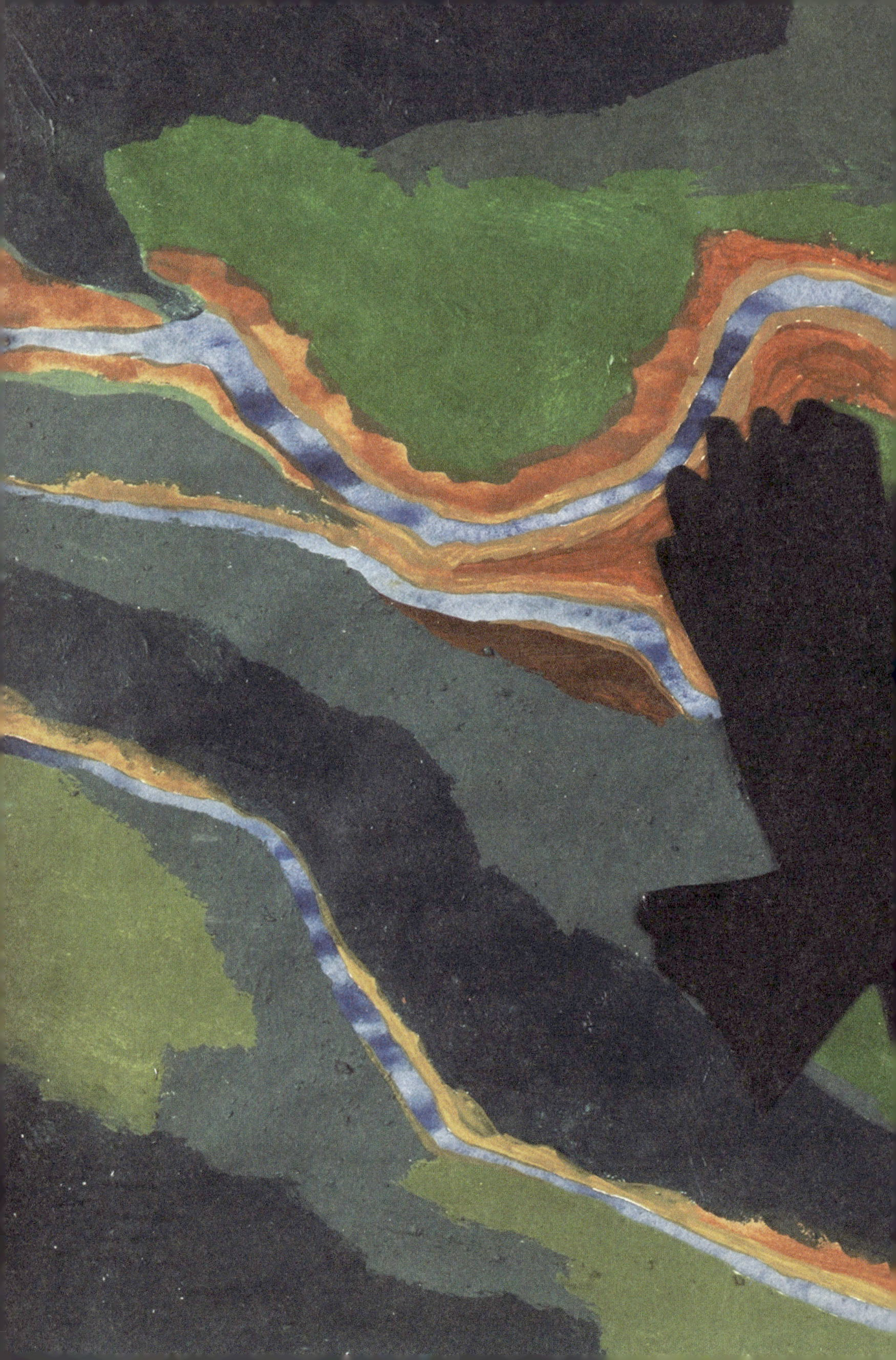

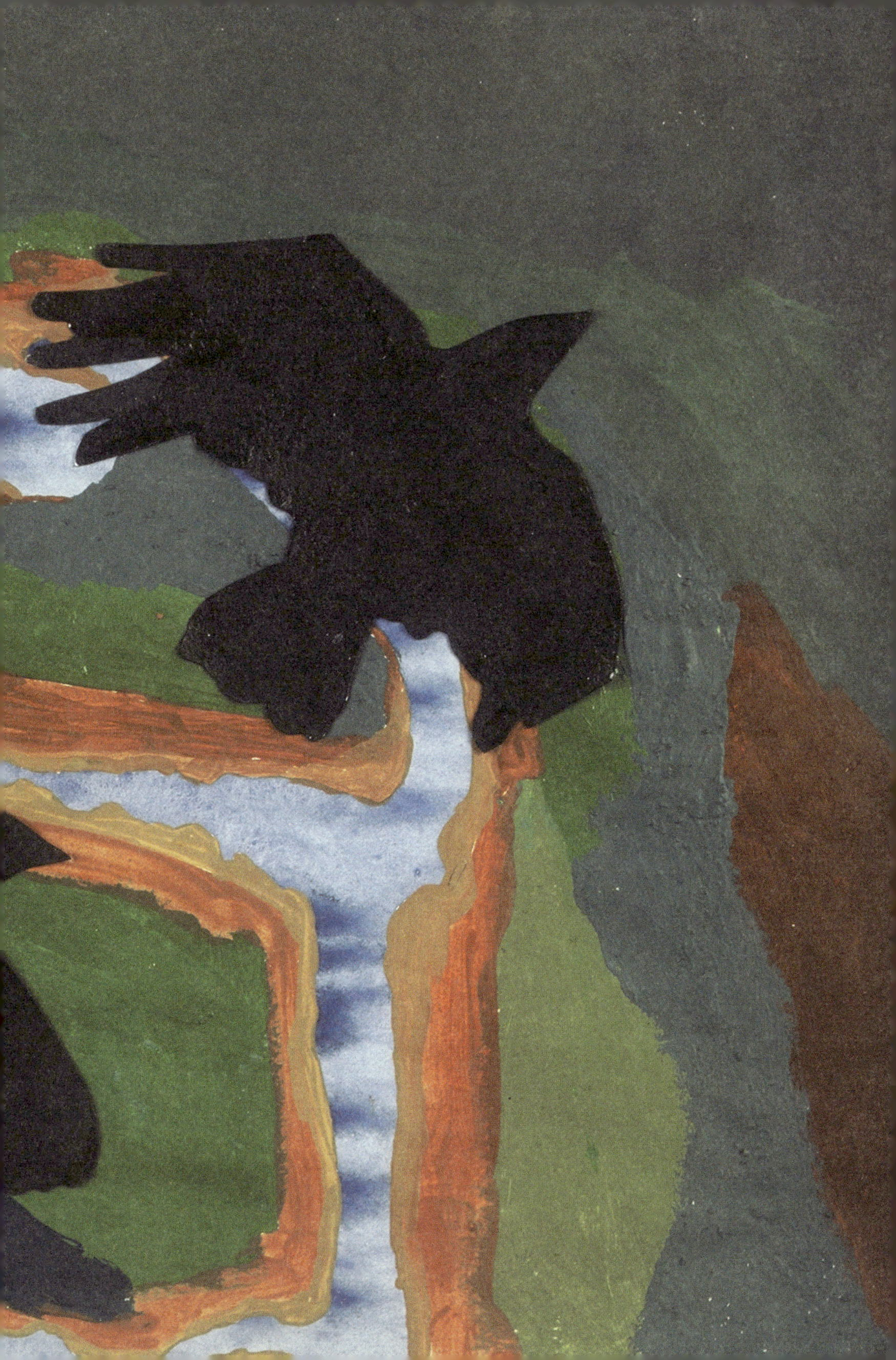

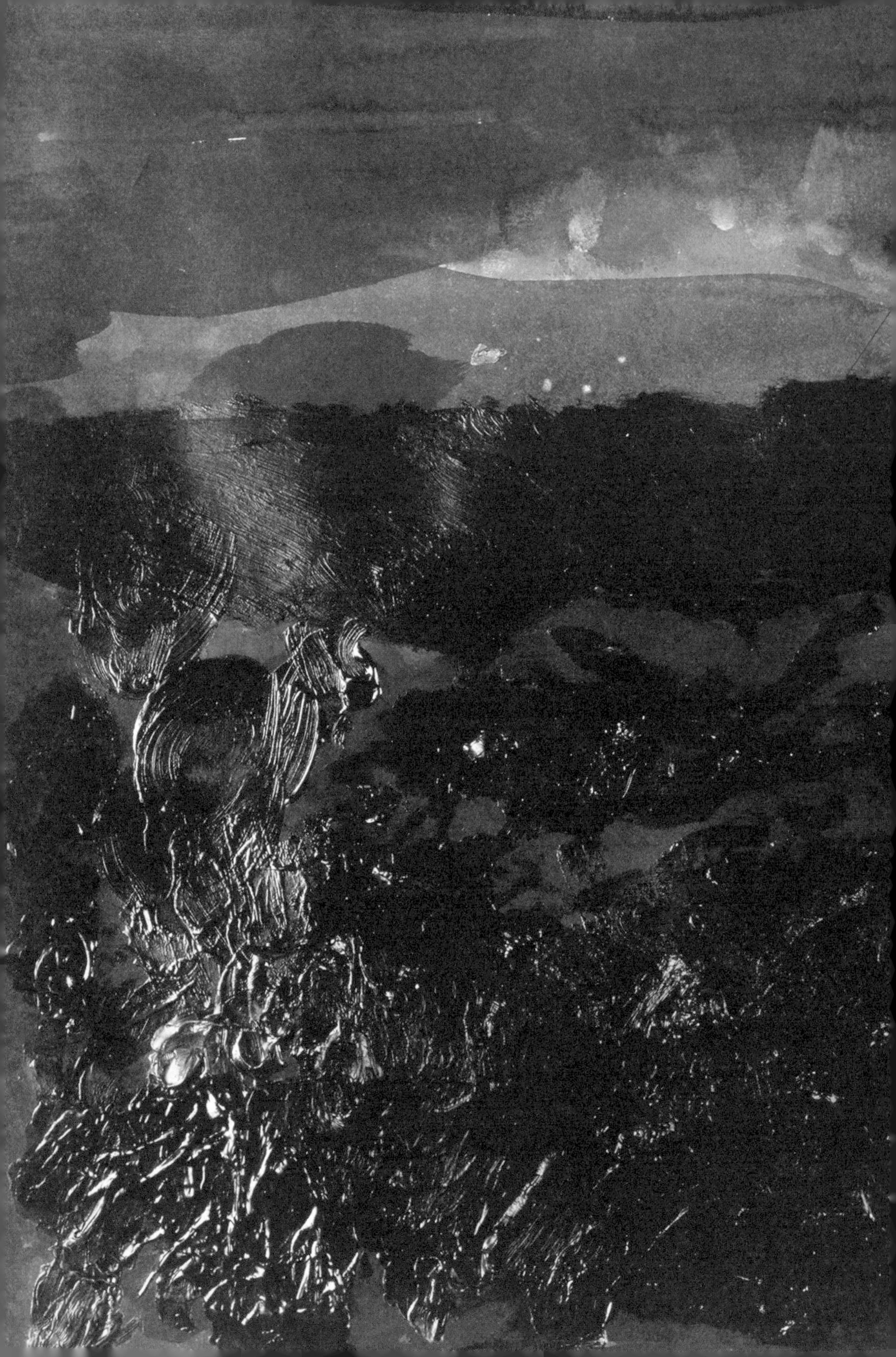

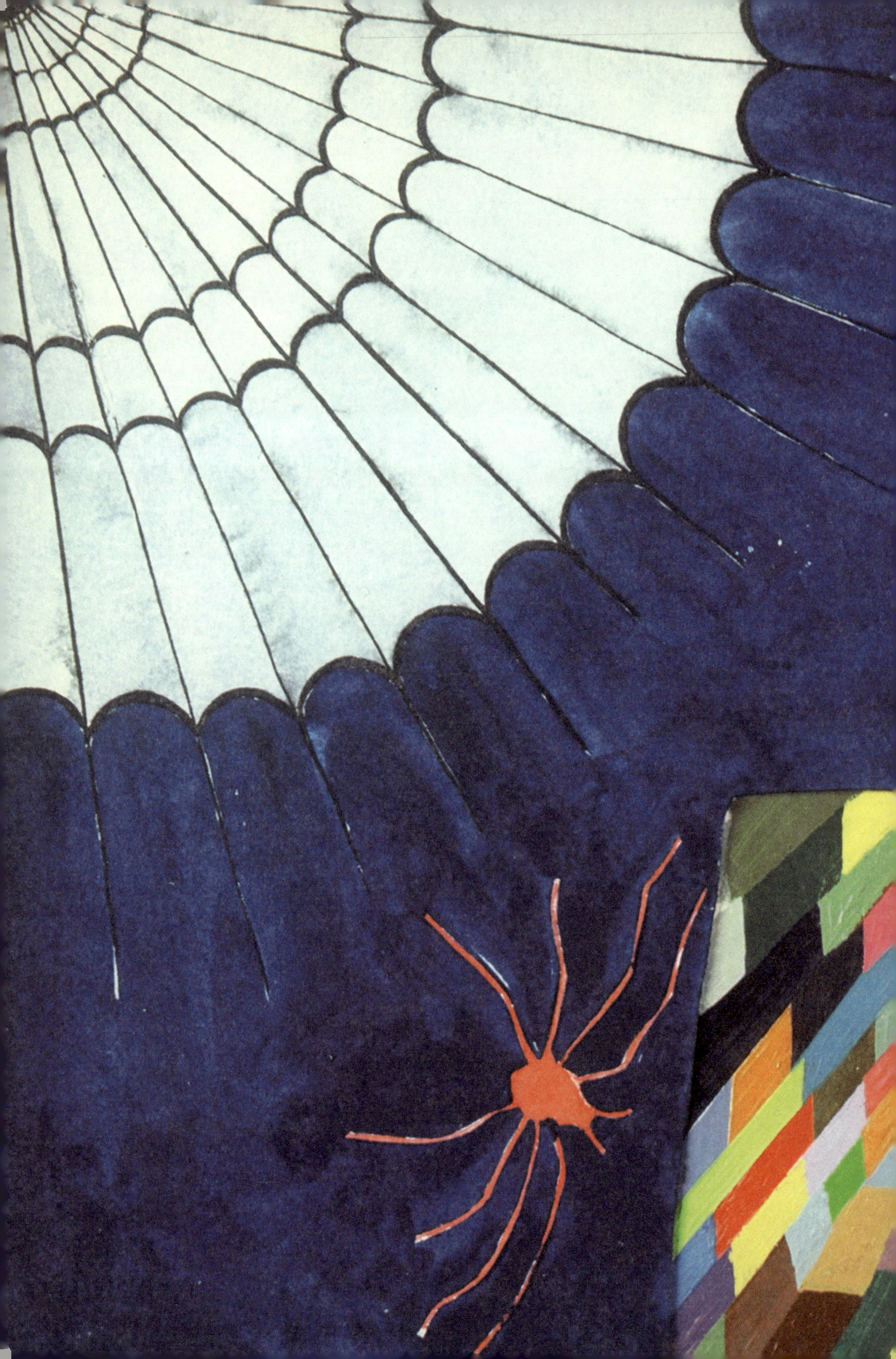

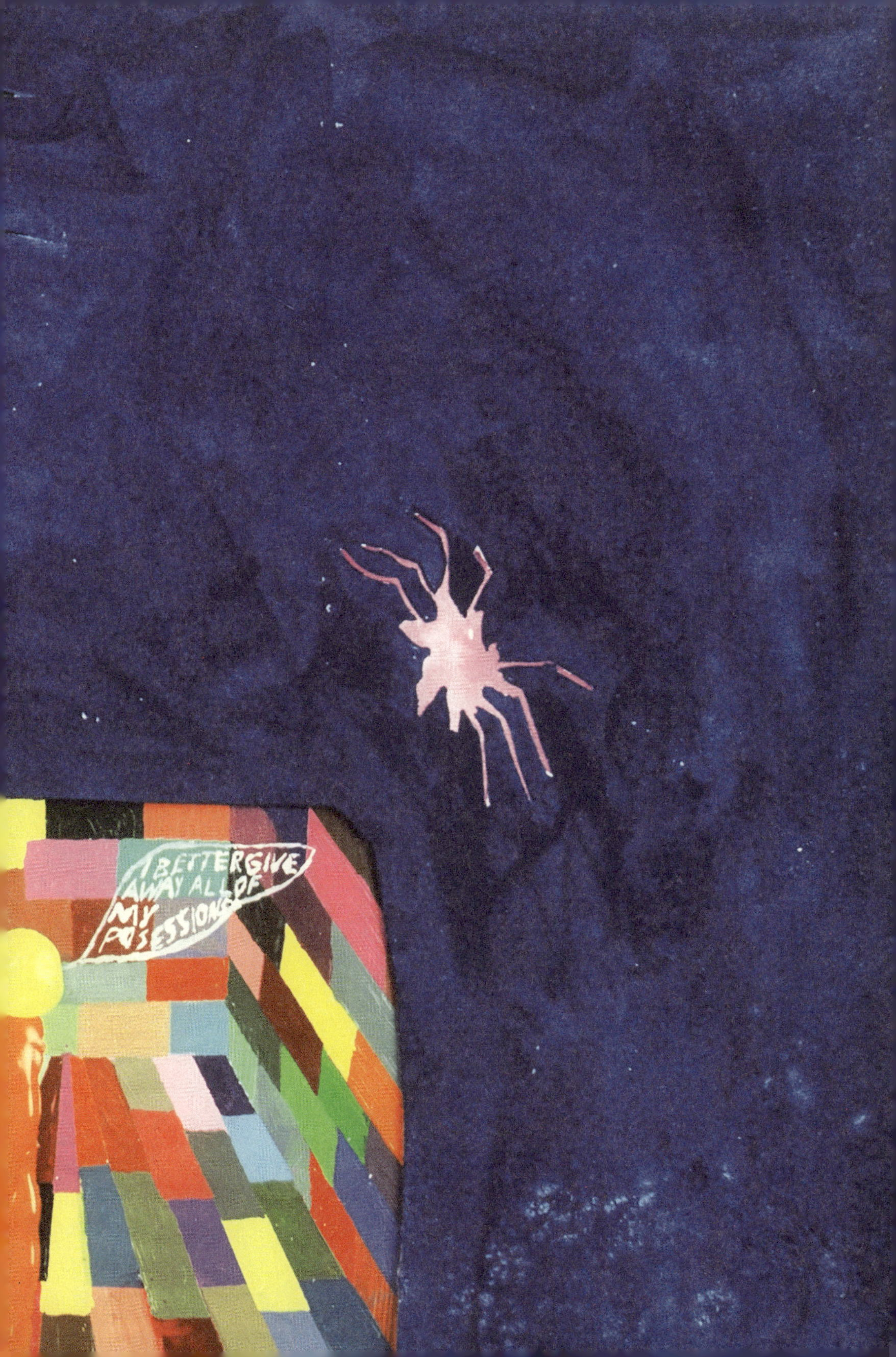
I BETTER GIVE
AWAY ALL OF
MY POSSESSIONS

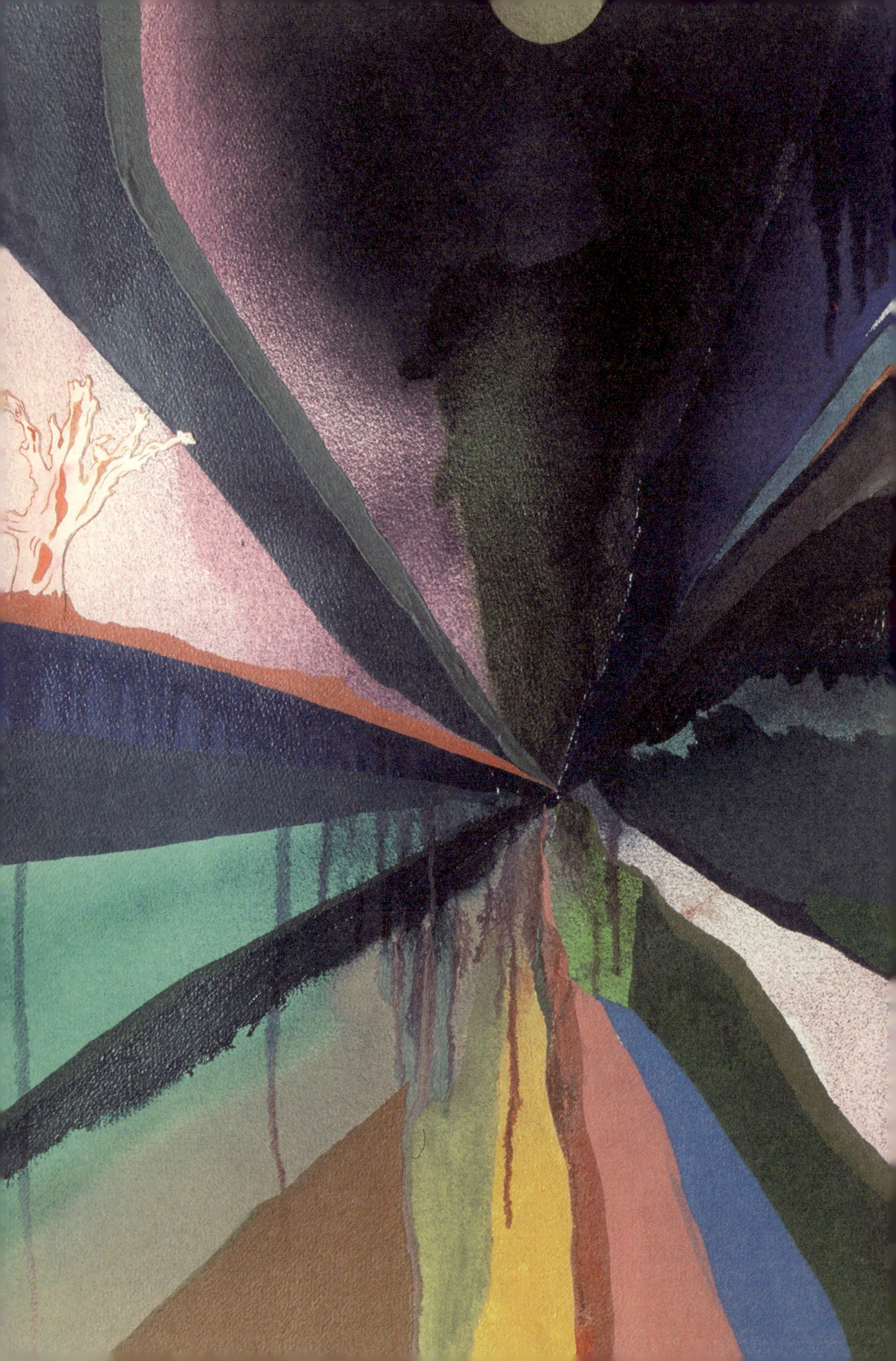

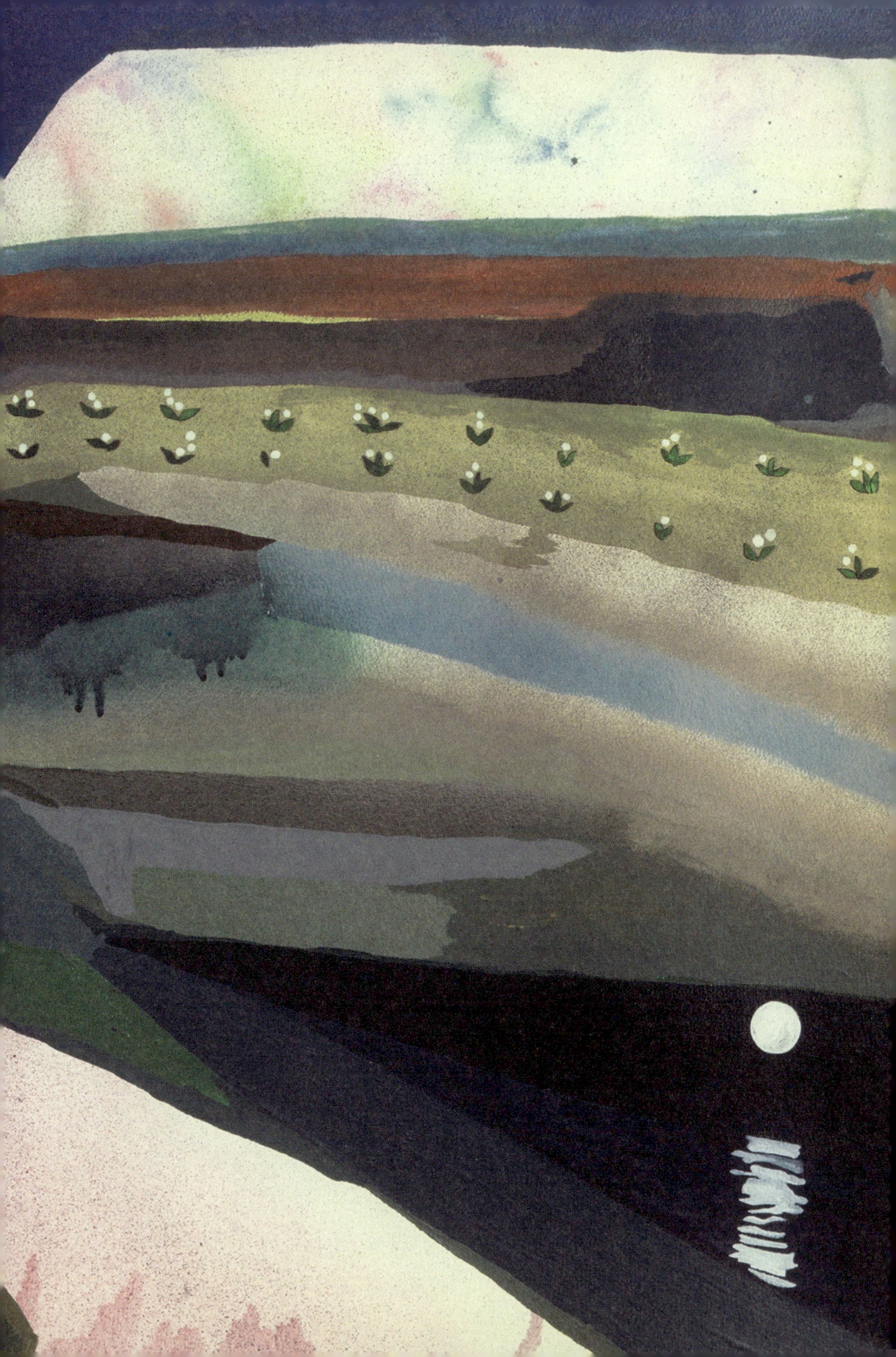

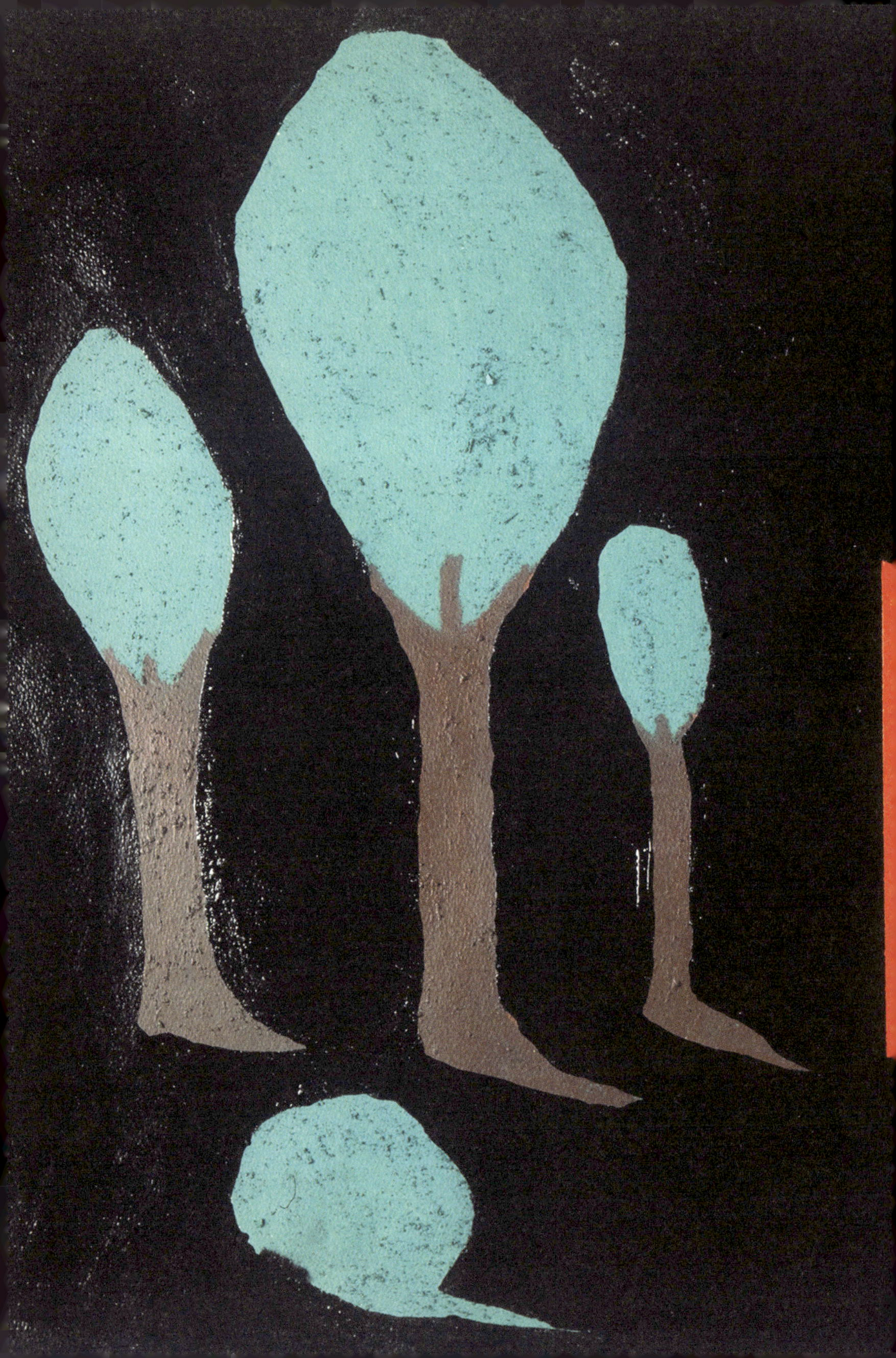

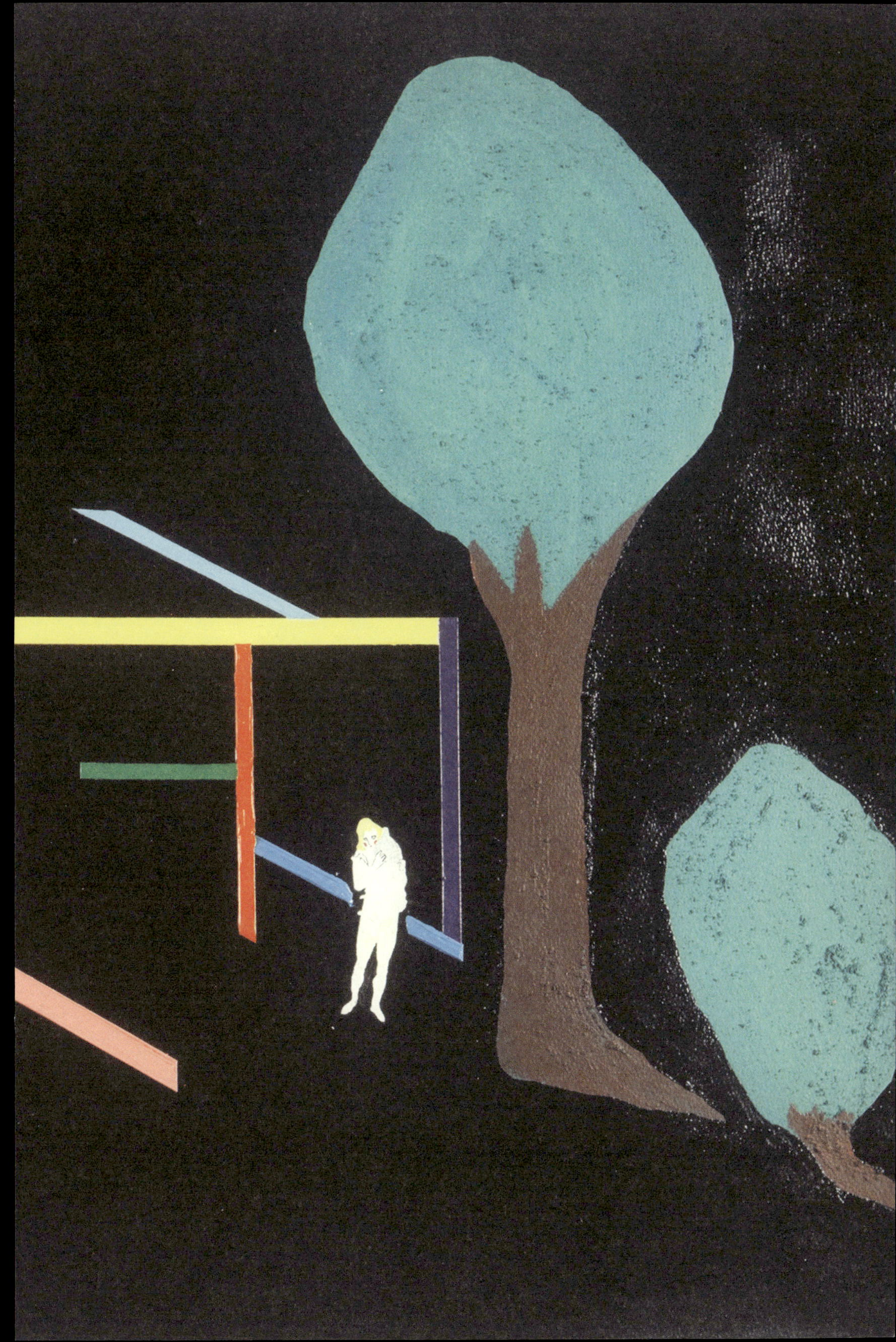

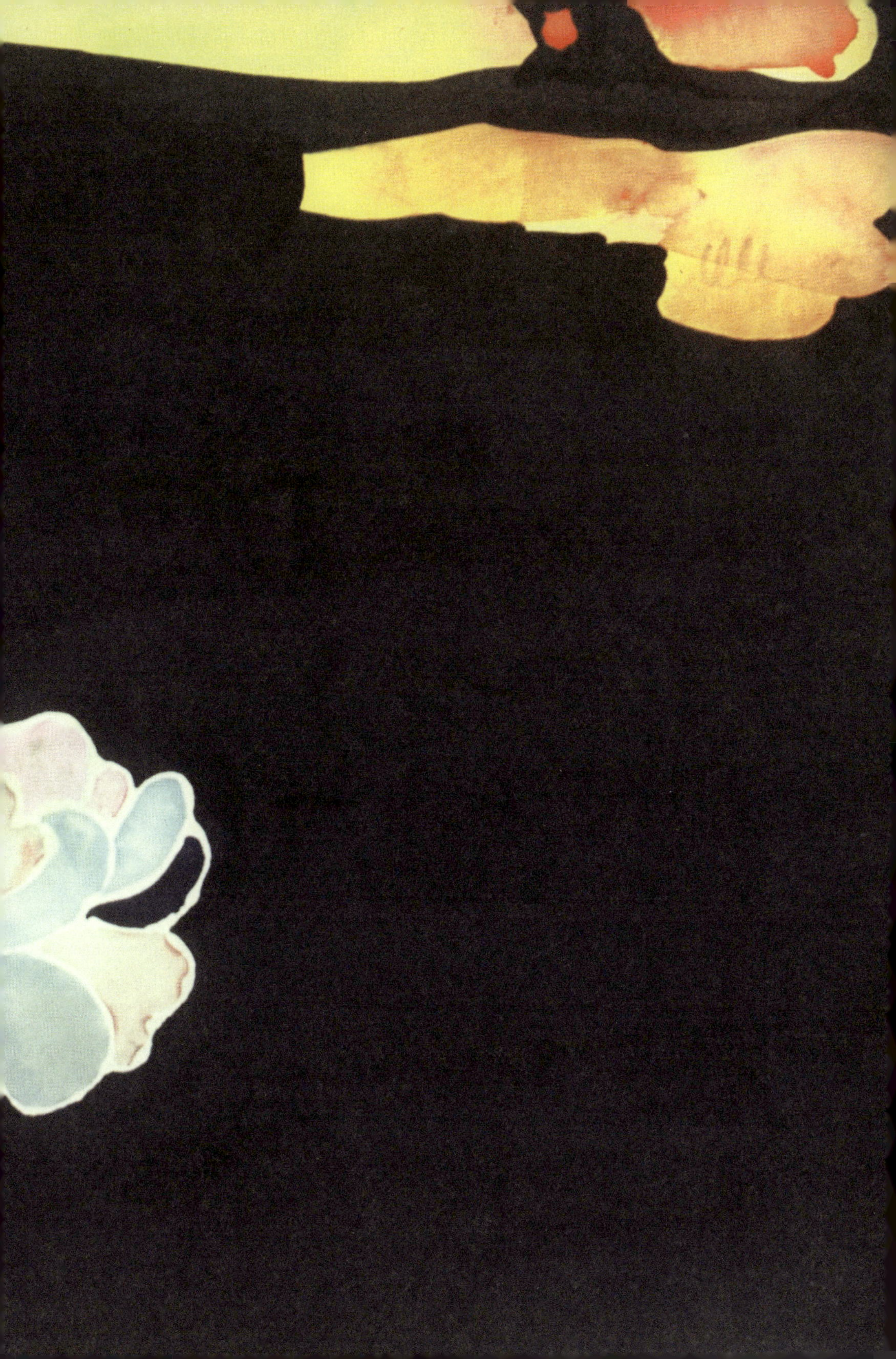

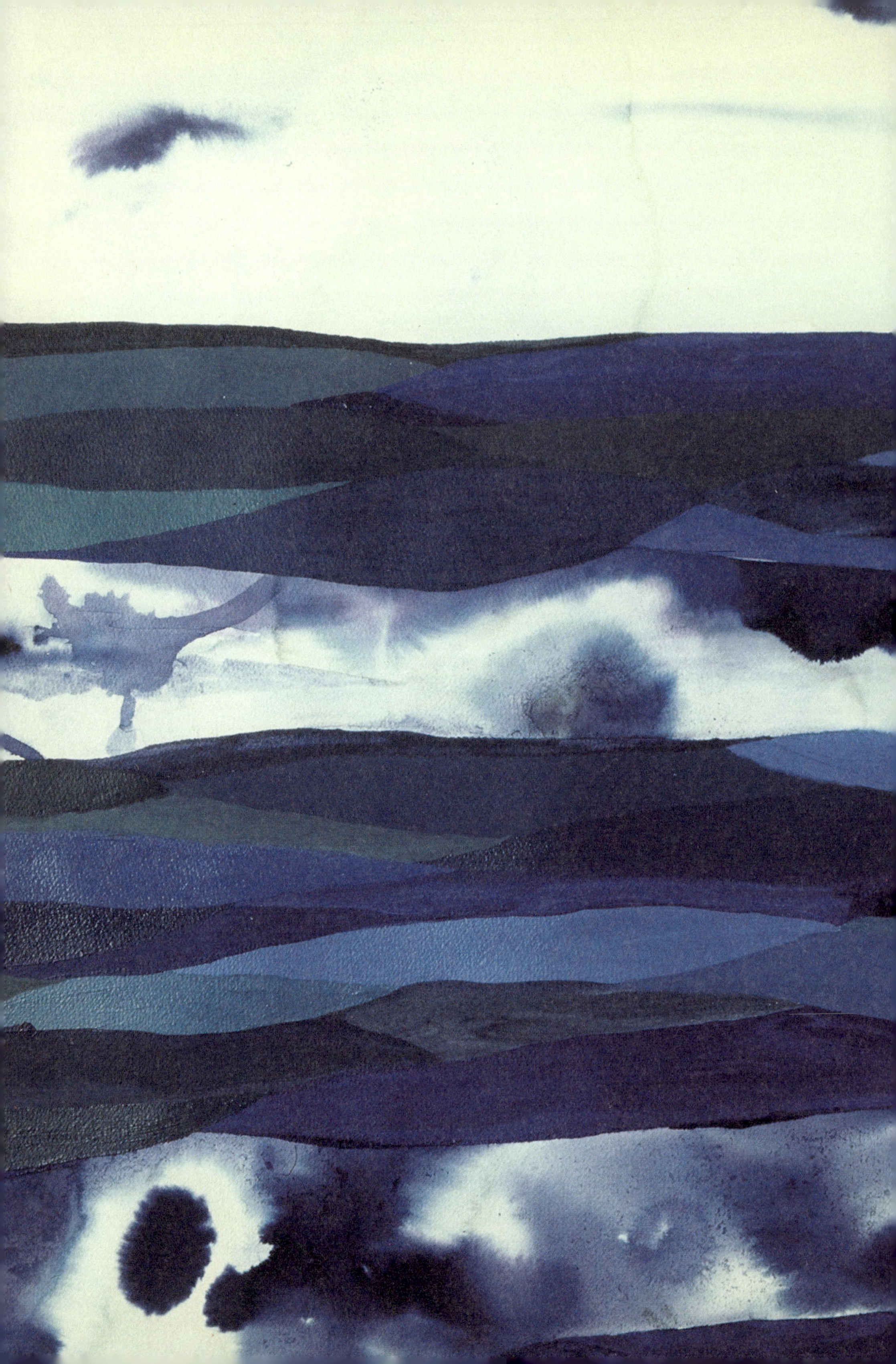

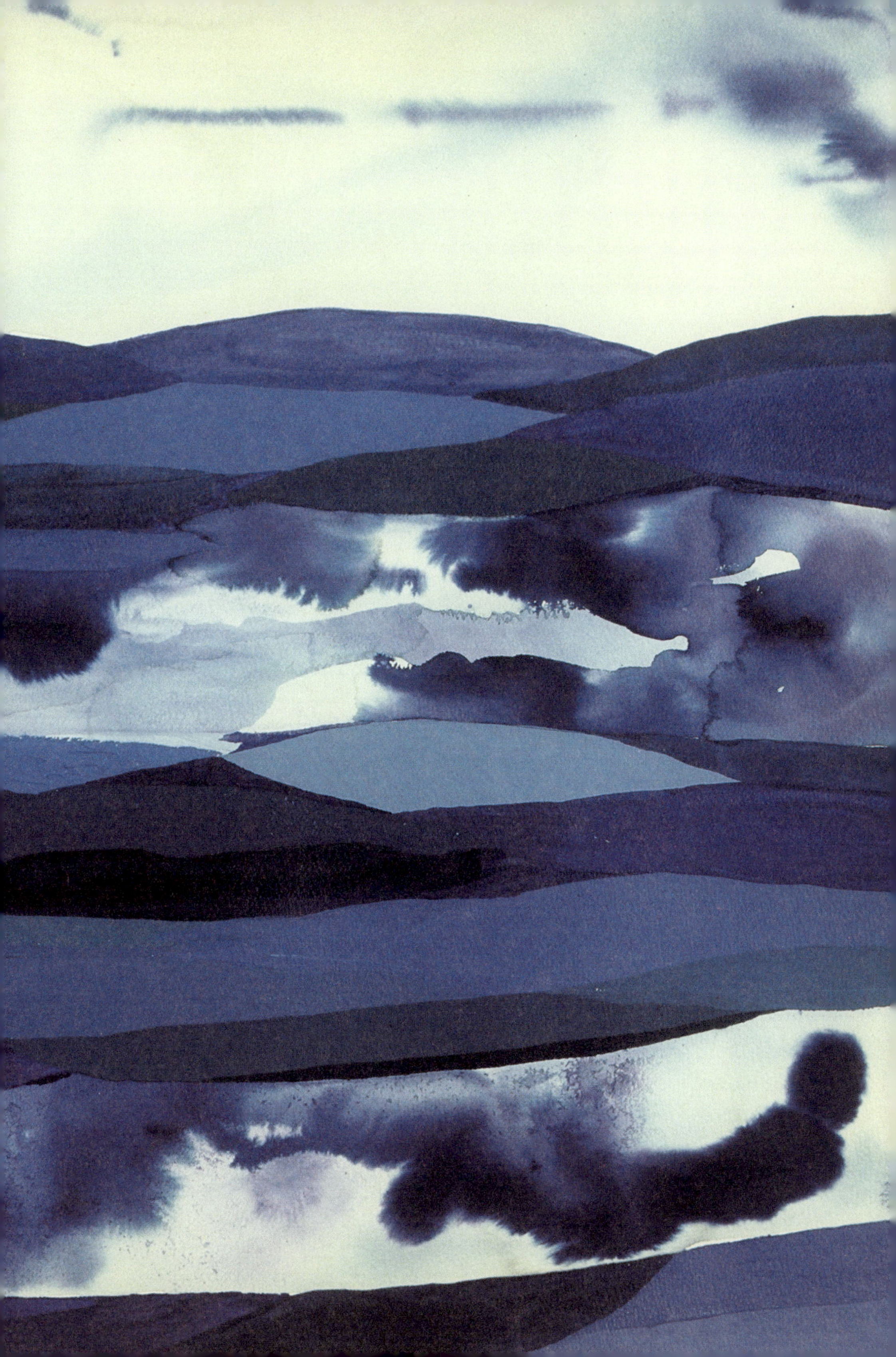

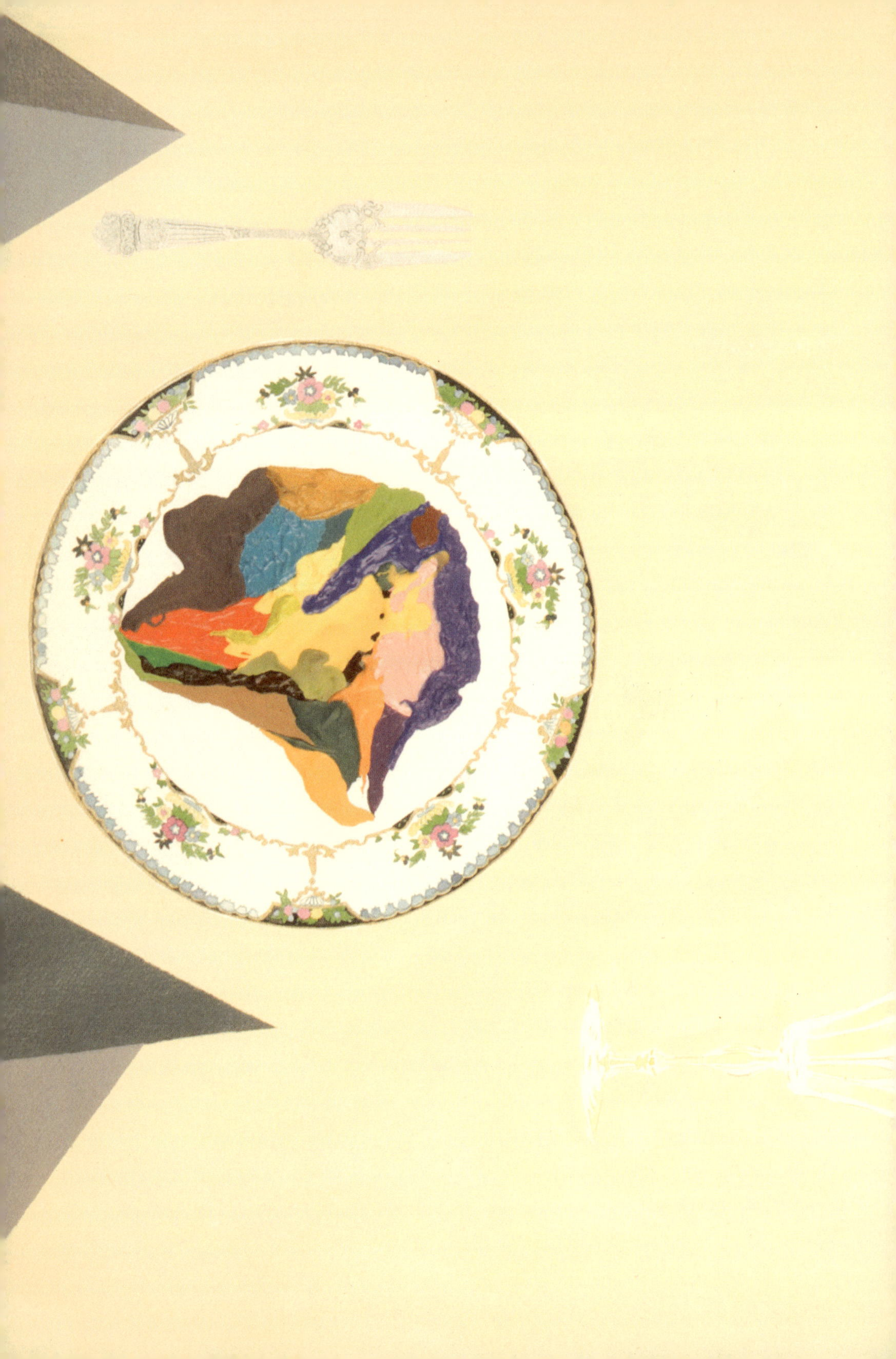

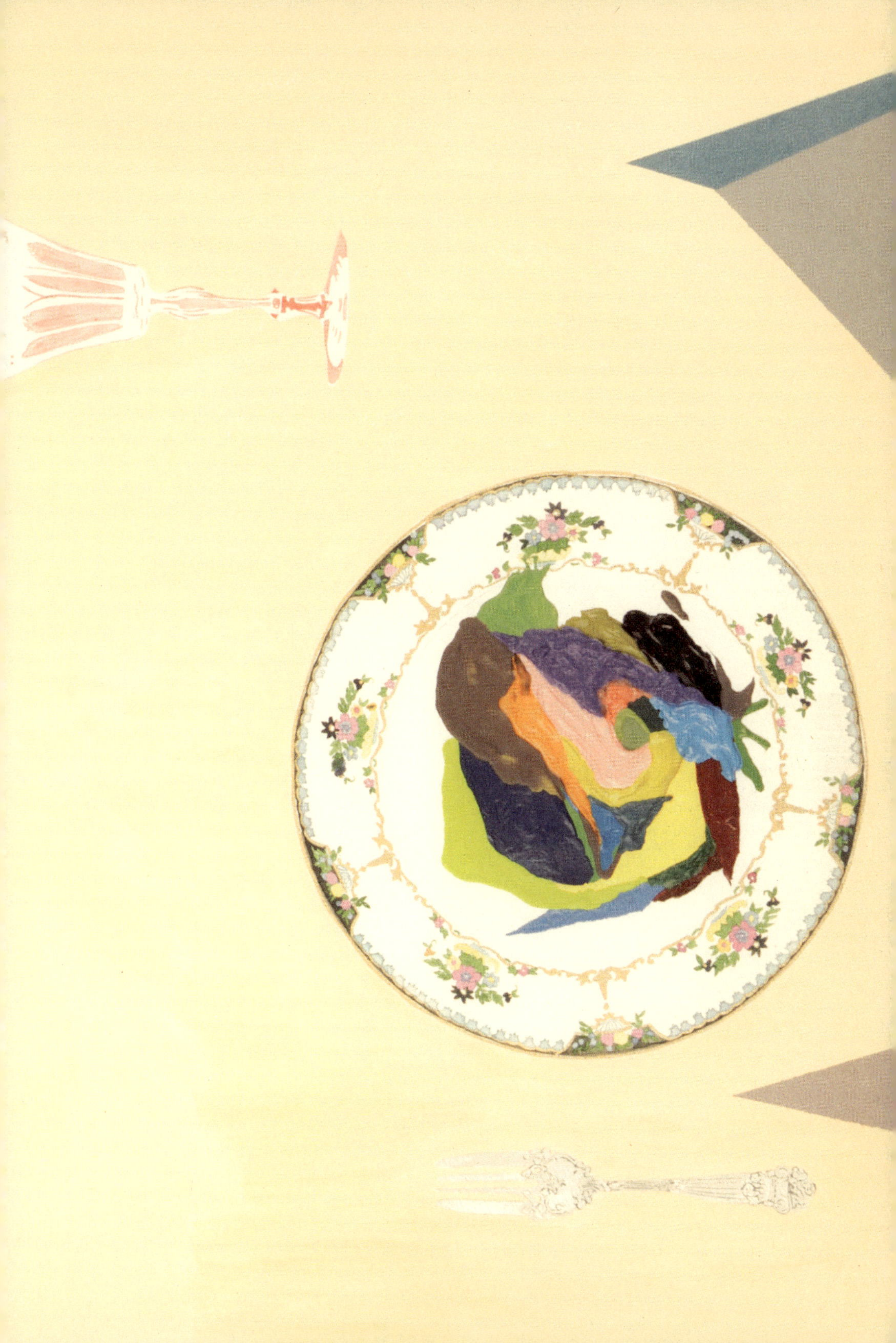

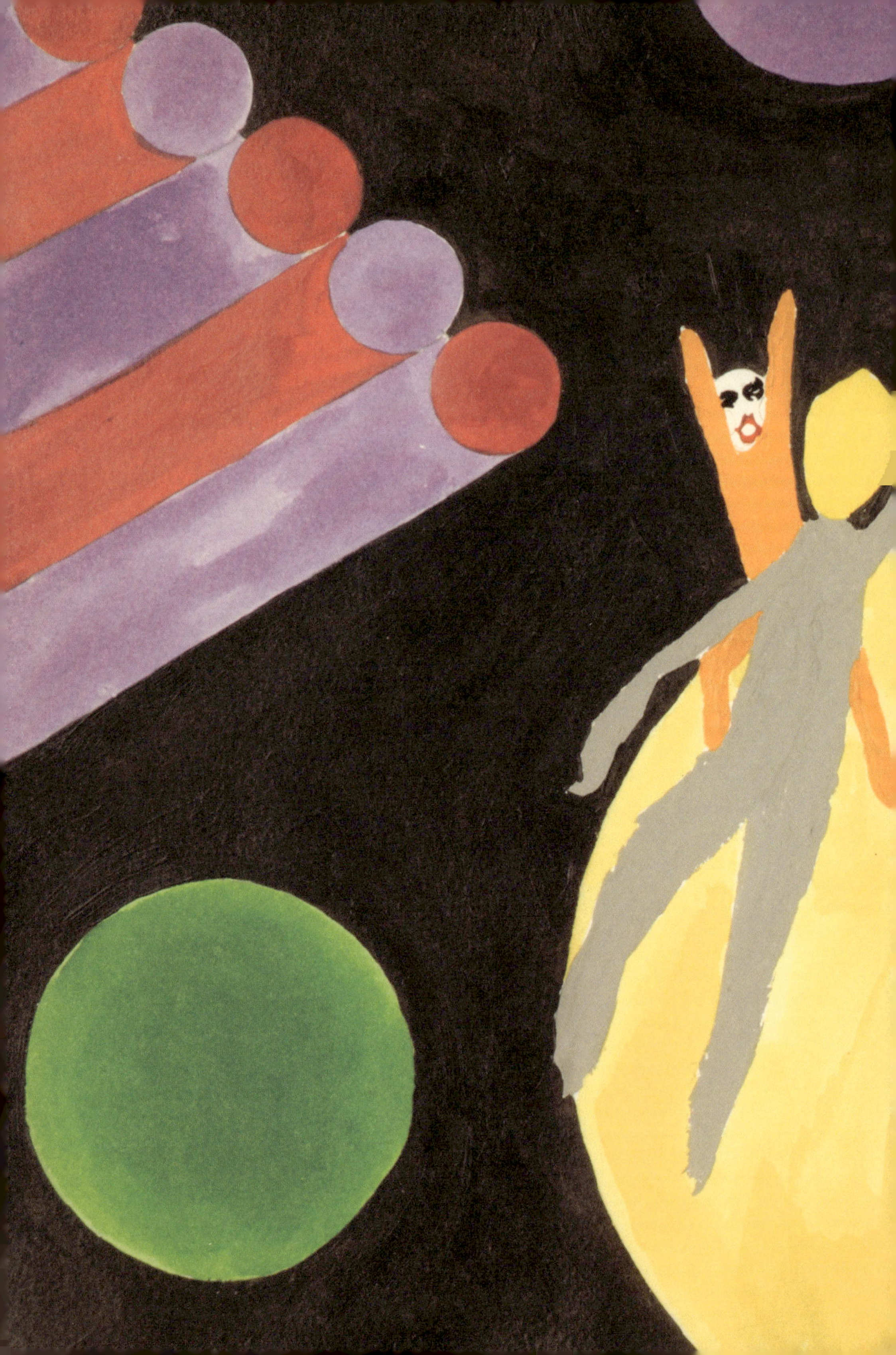

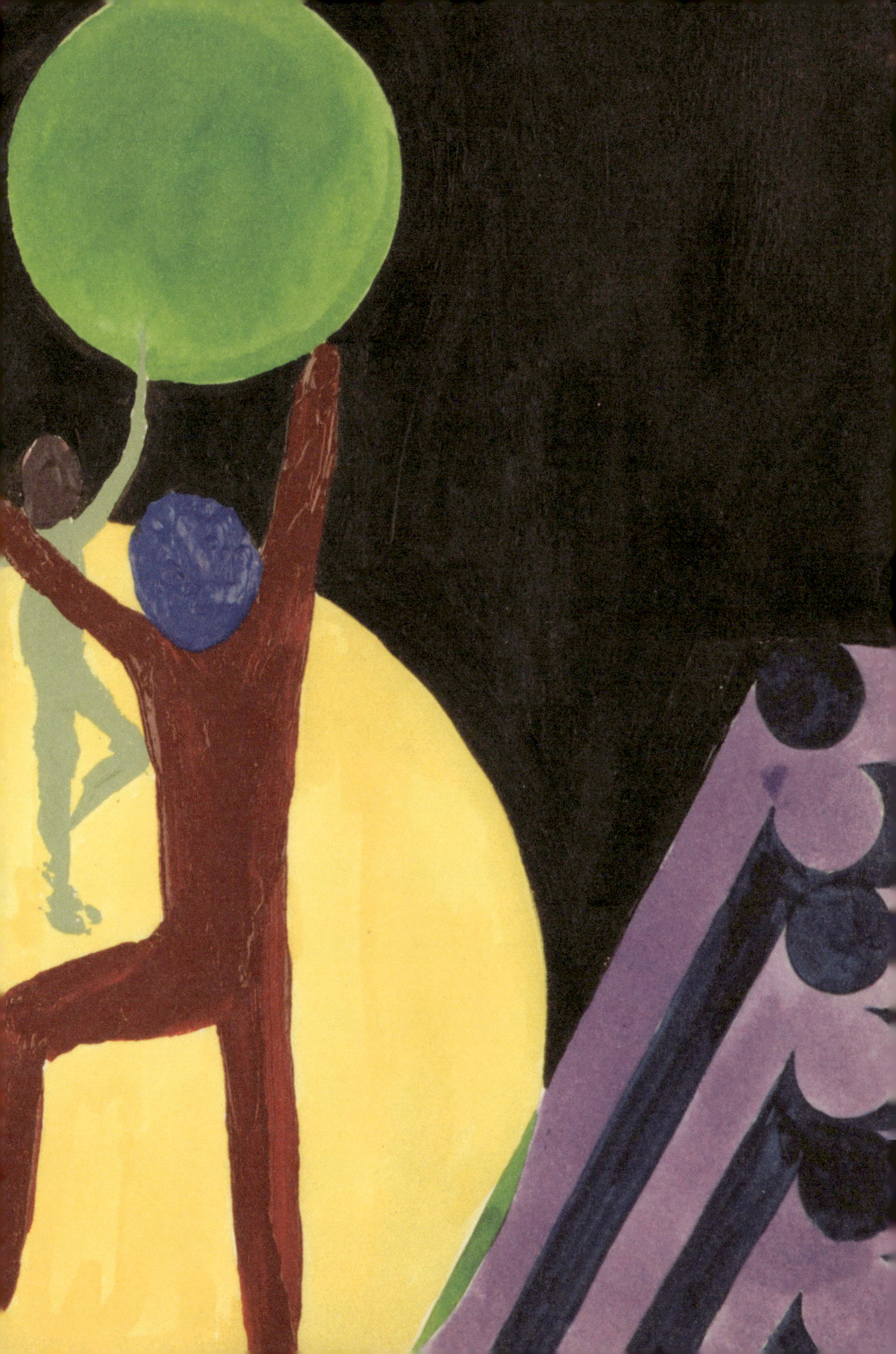

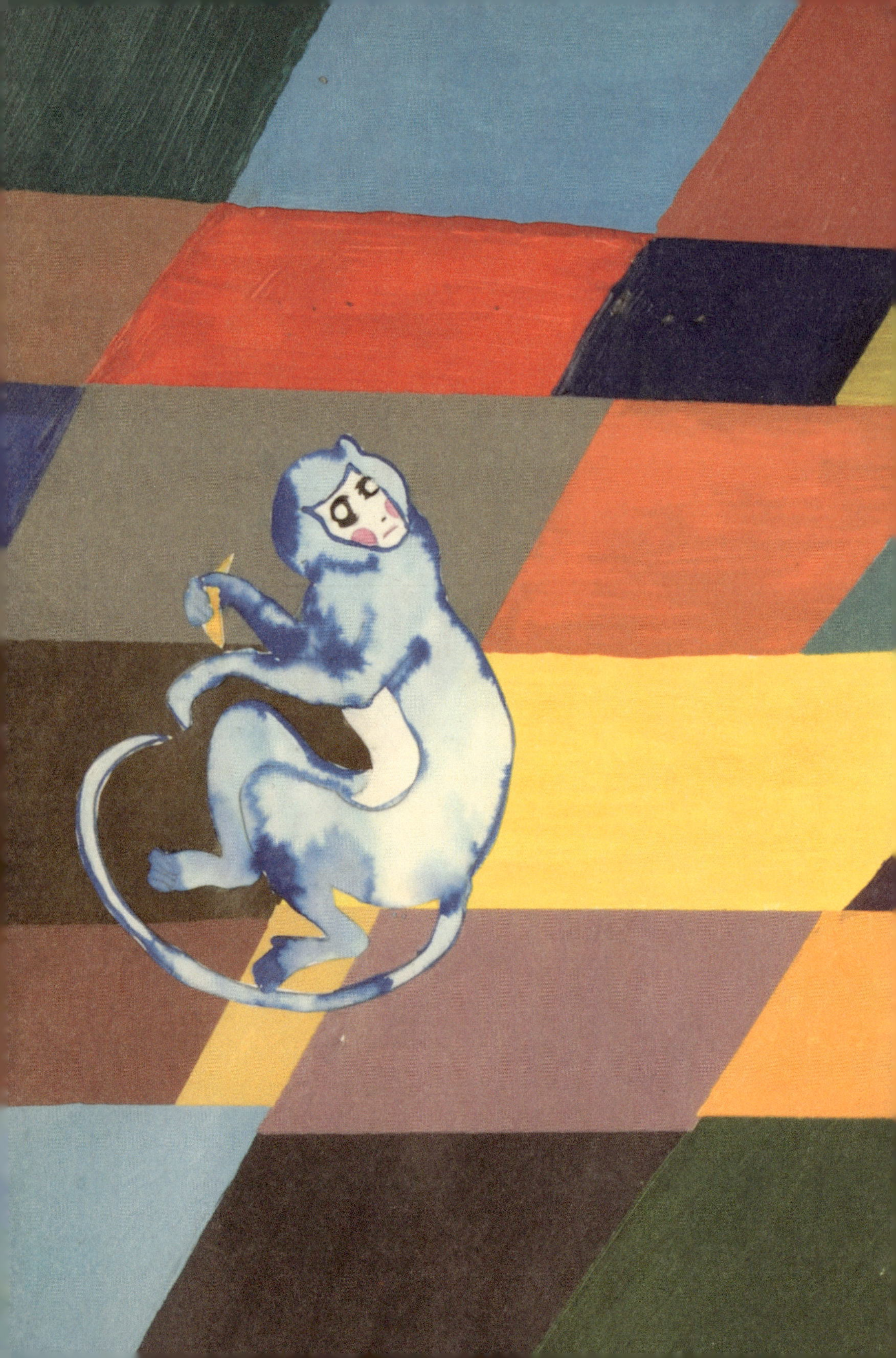

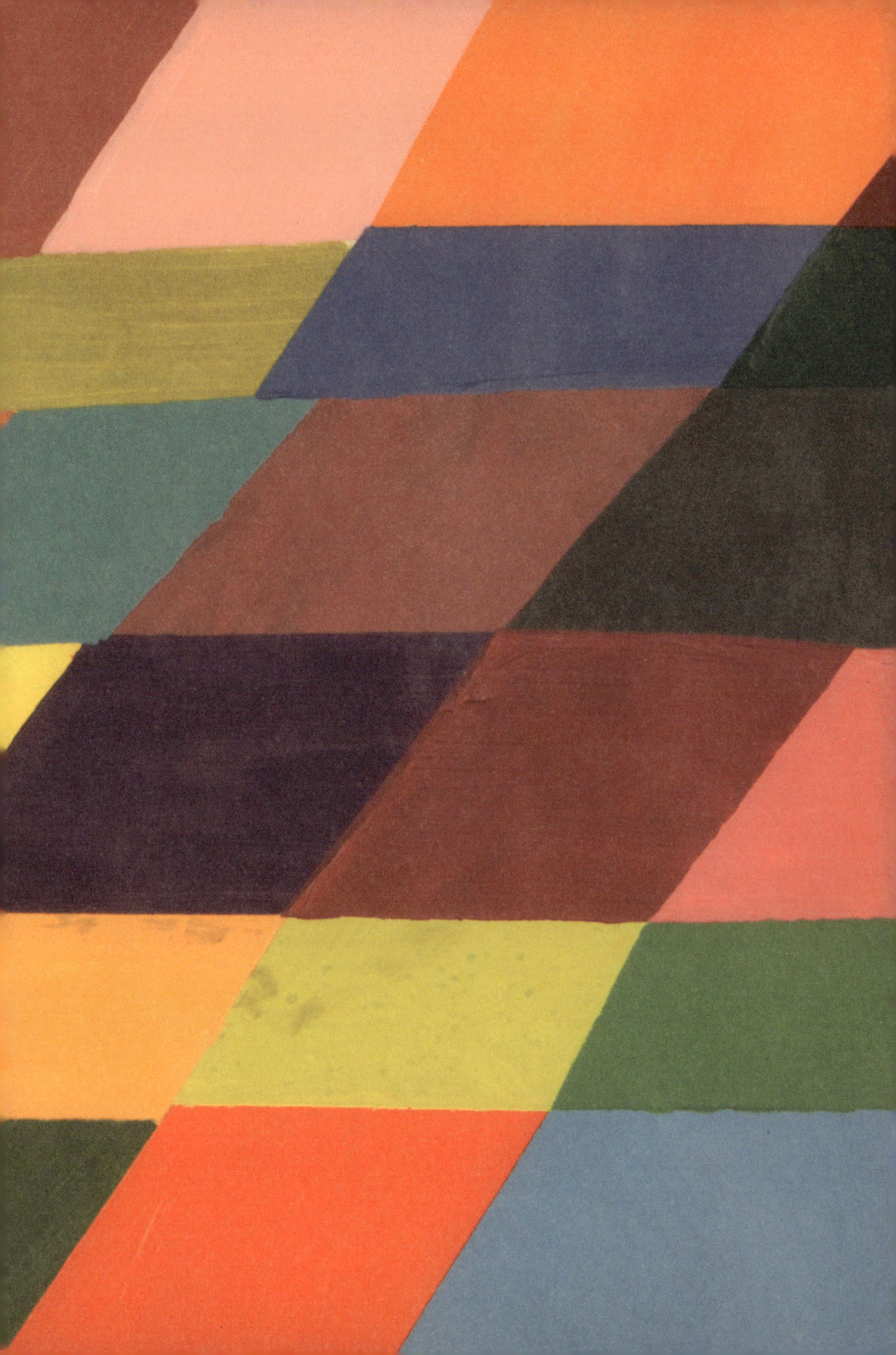

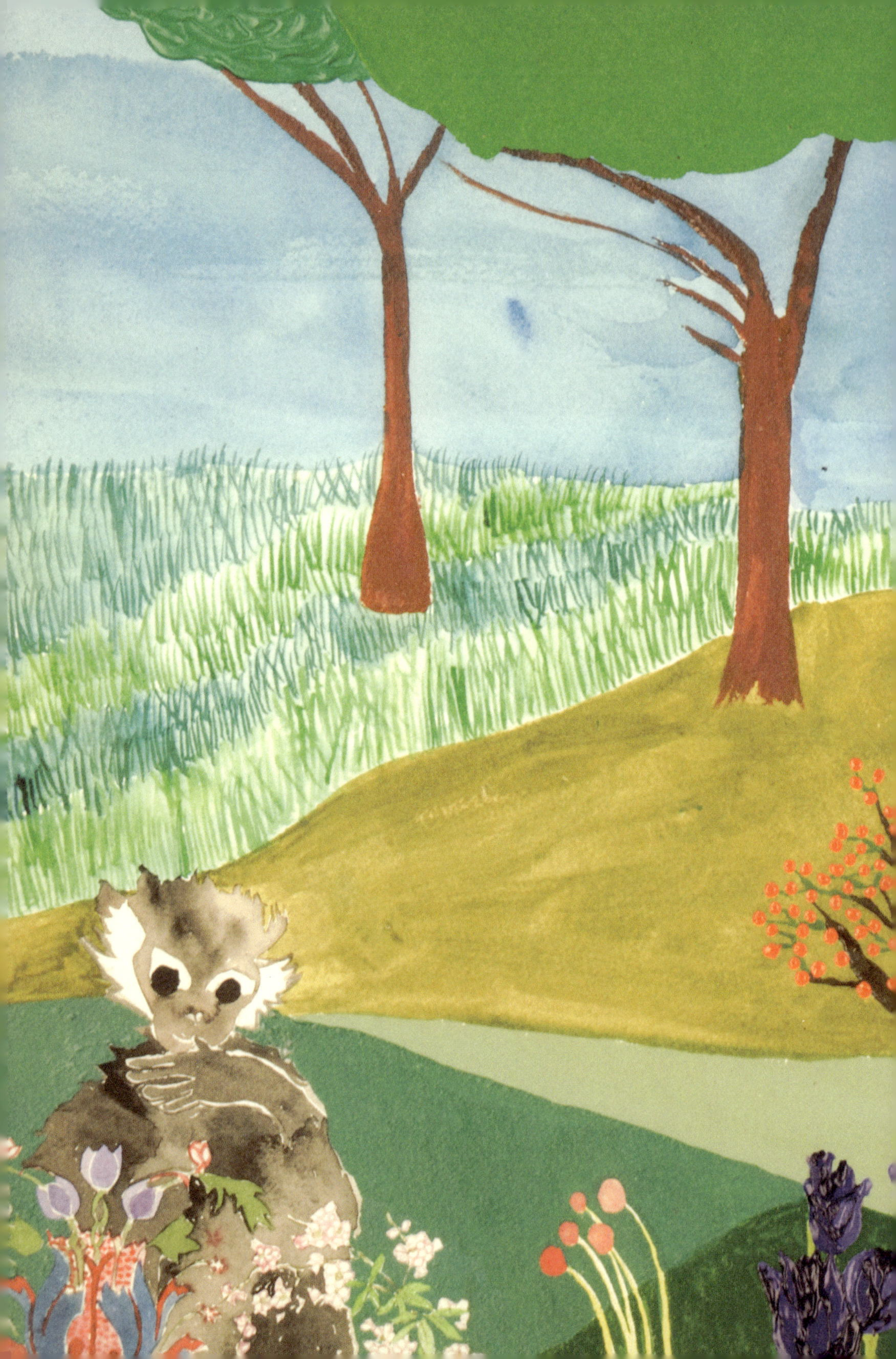

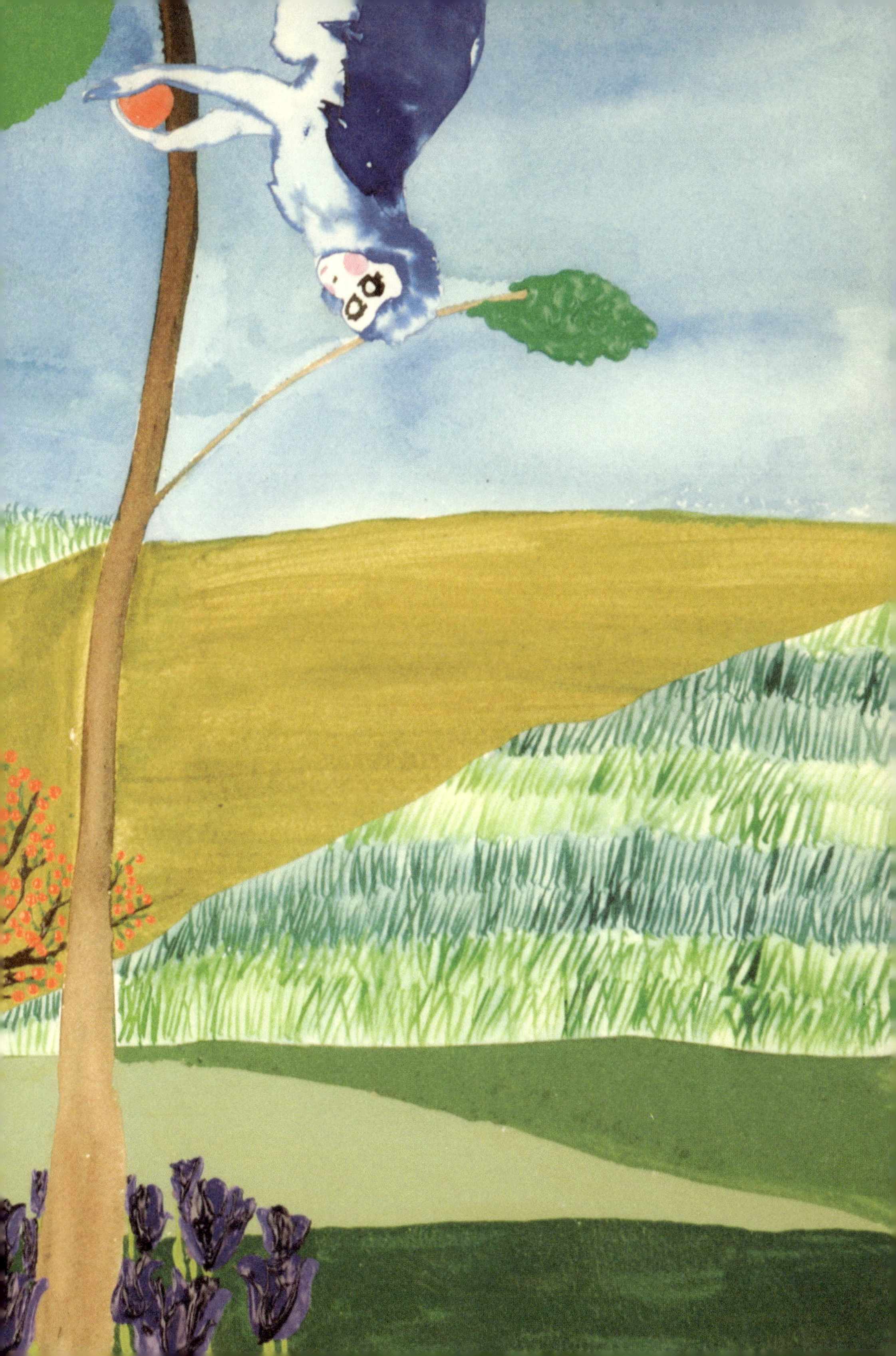

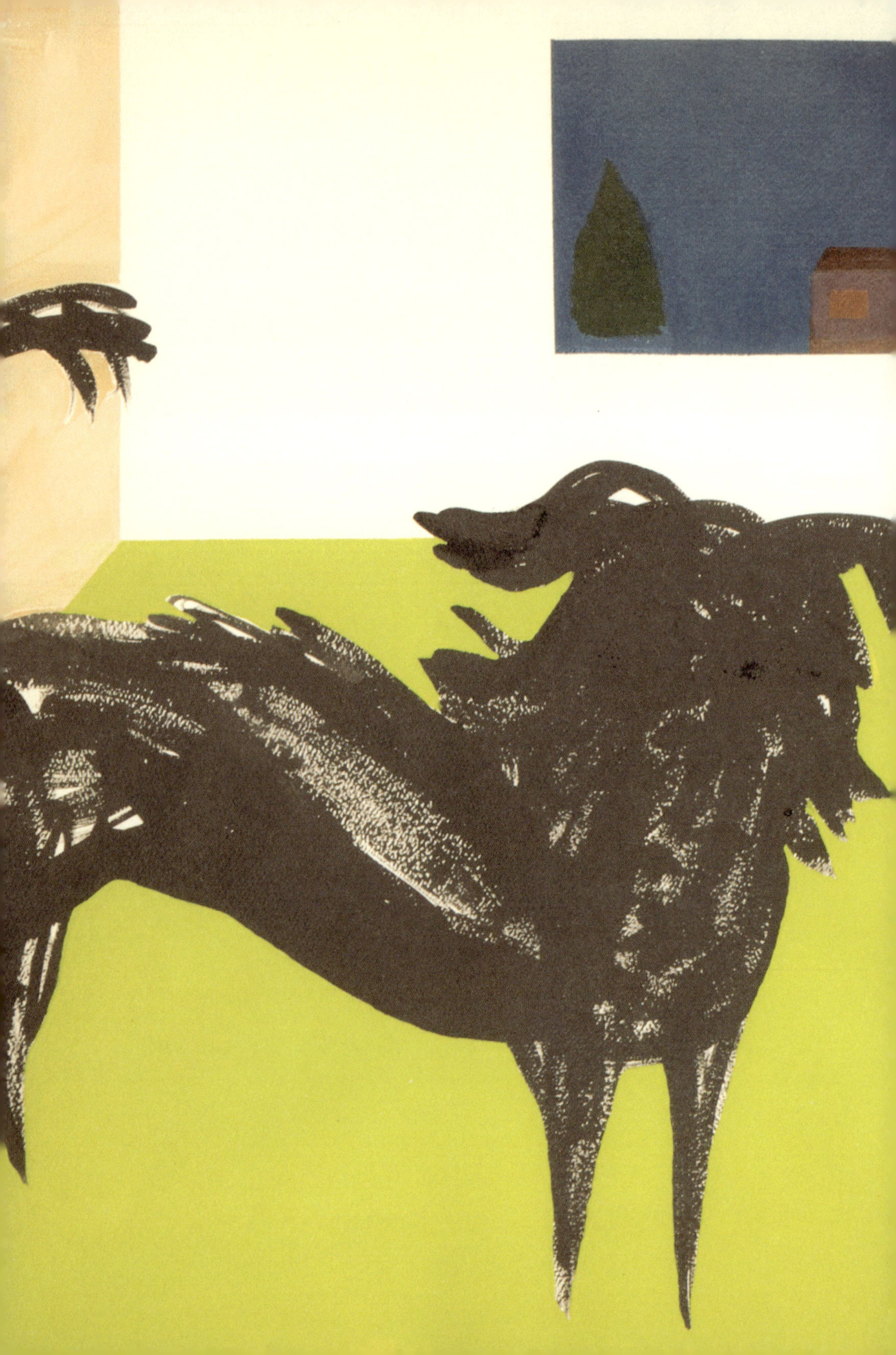

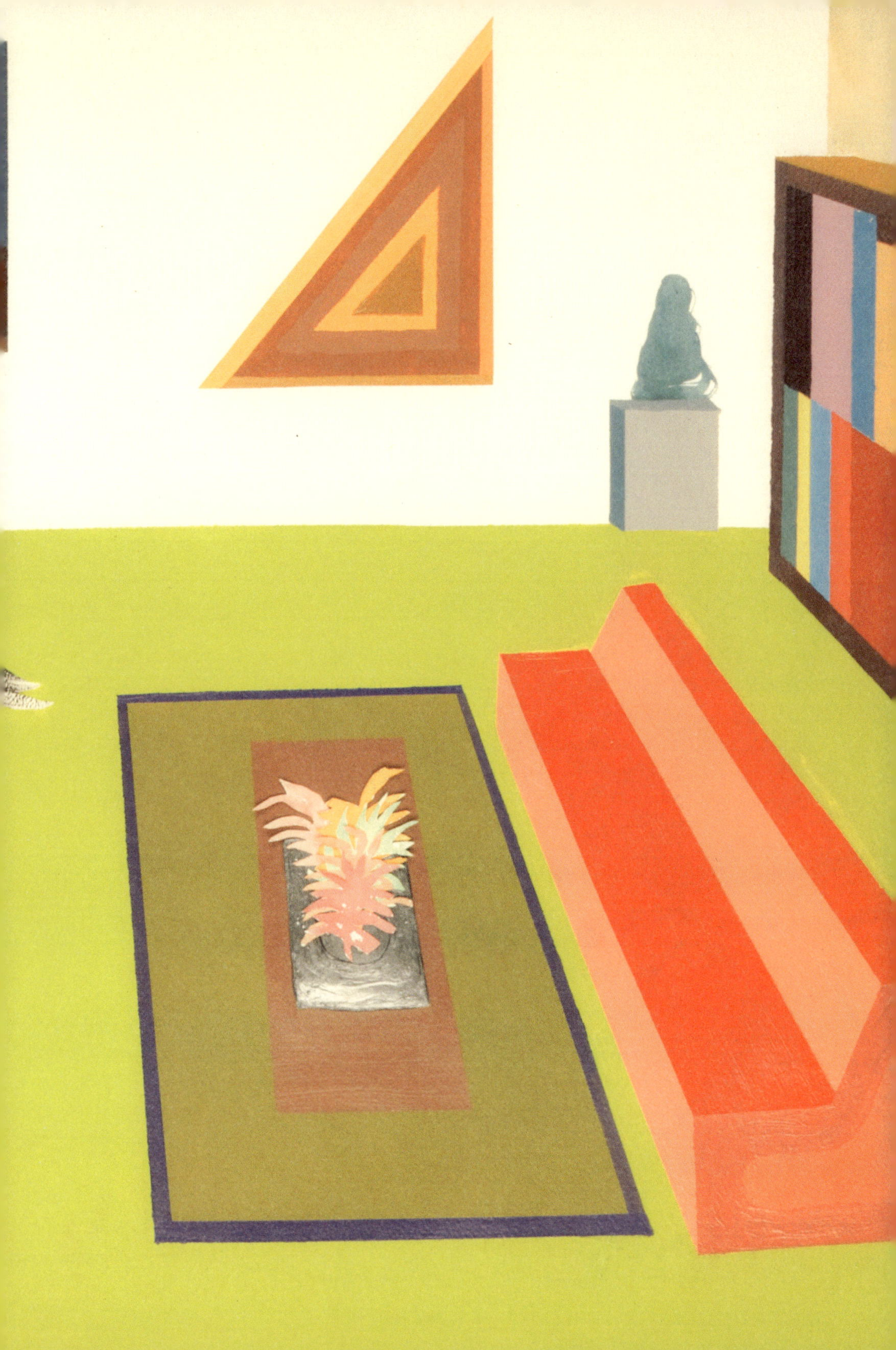

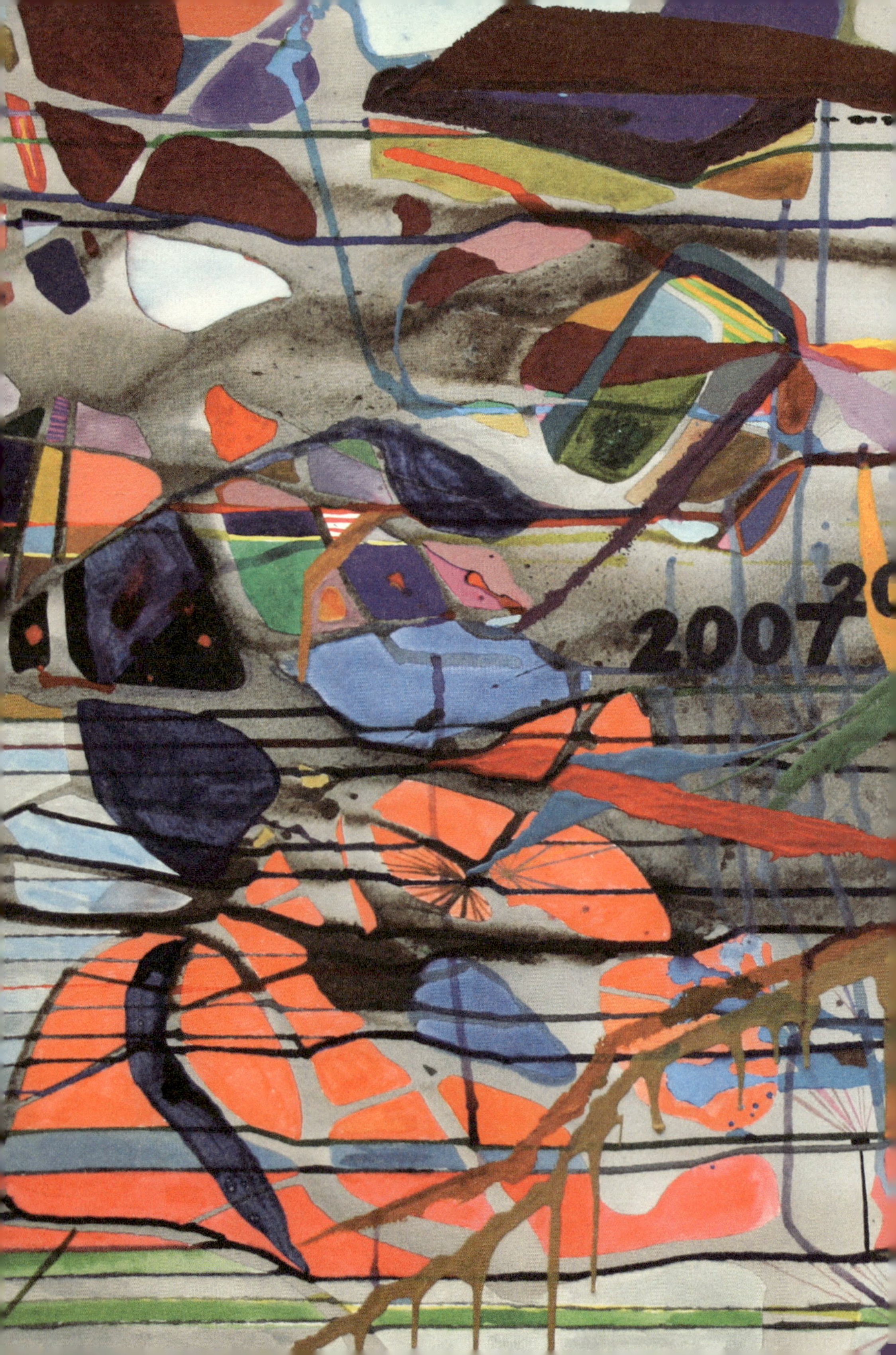
2007

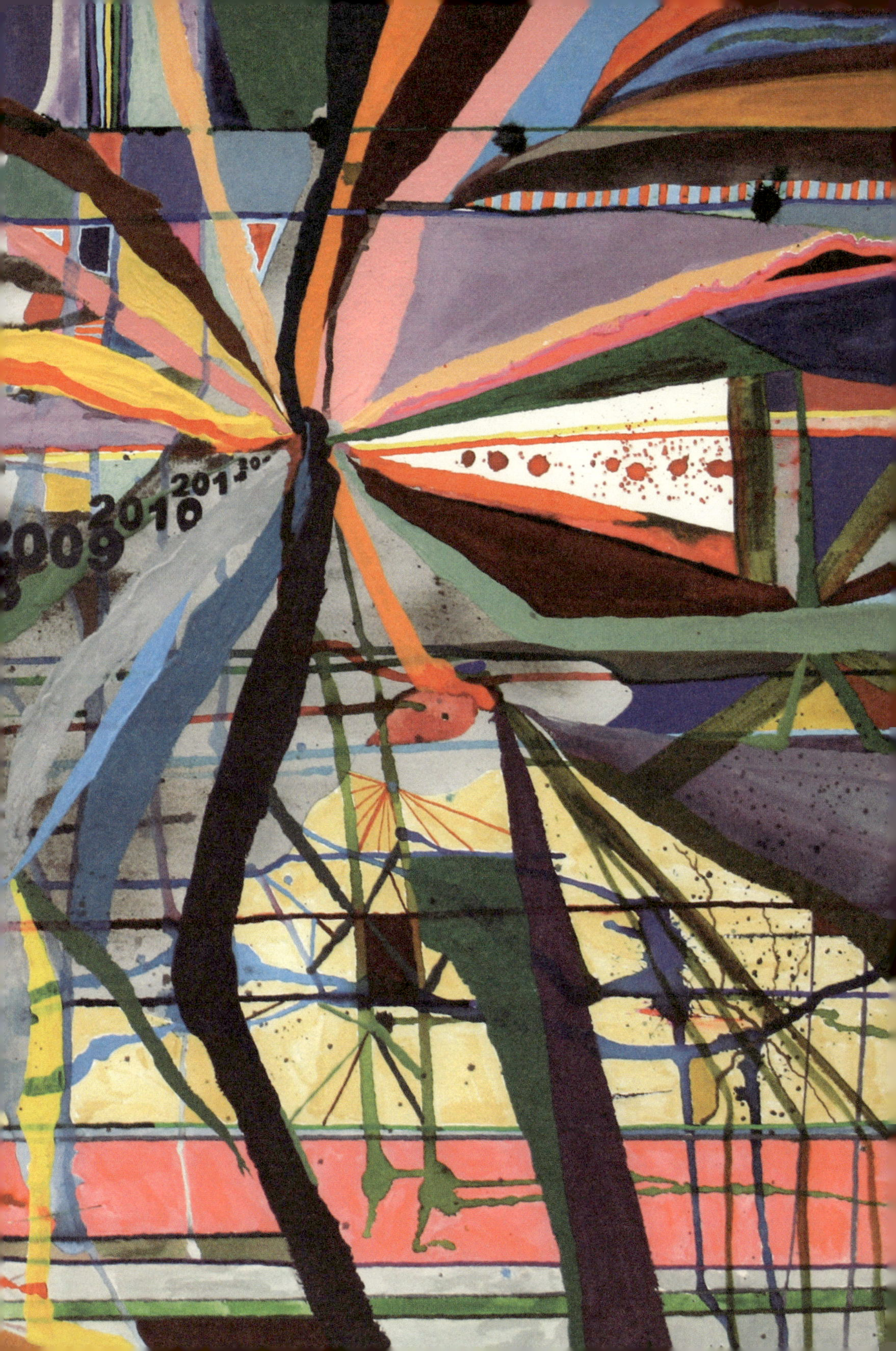

2009
2010
201

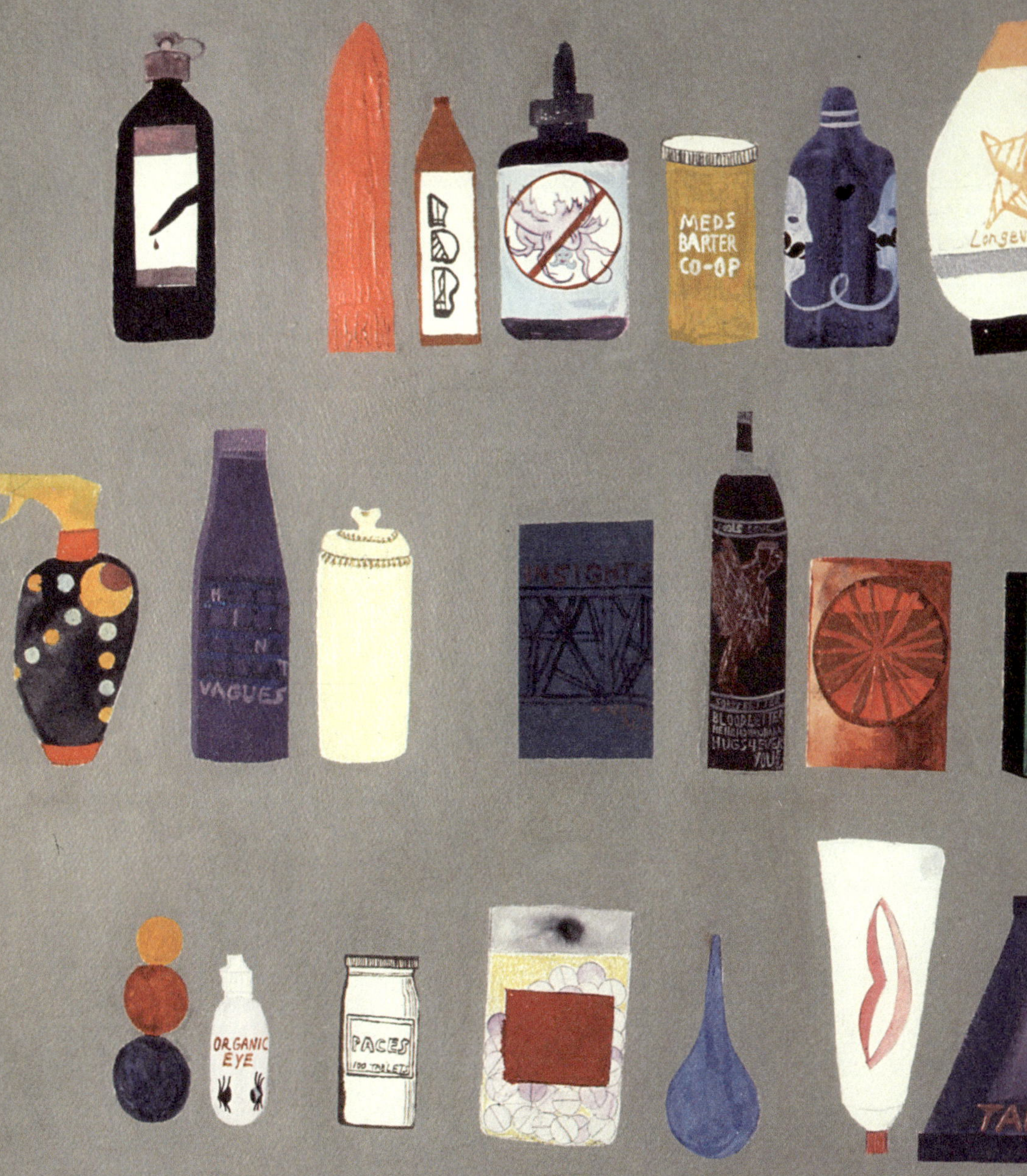
MEDS
BARTER
CO-OP
Longevi
VAGUES
INSIGHT
BLOODLETTER
HUGS4EVER
YOU
ORGANIC
EYE
PACES
100 TABLETS
TAM

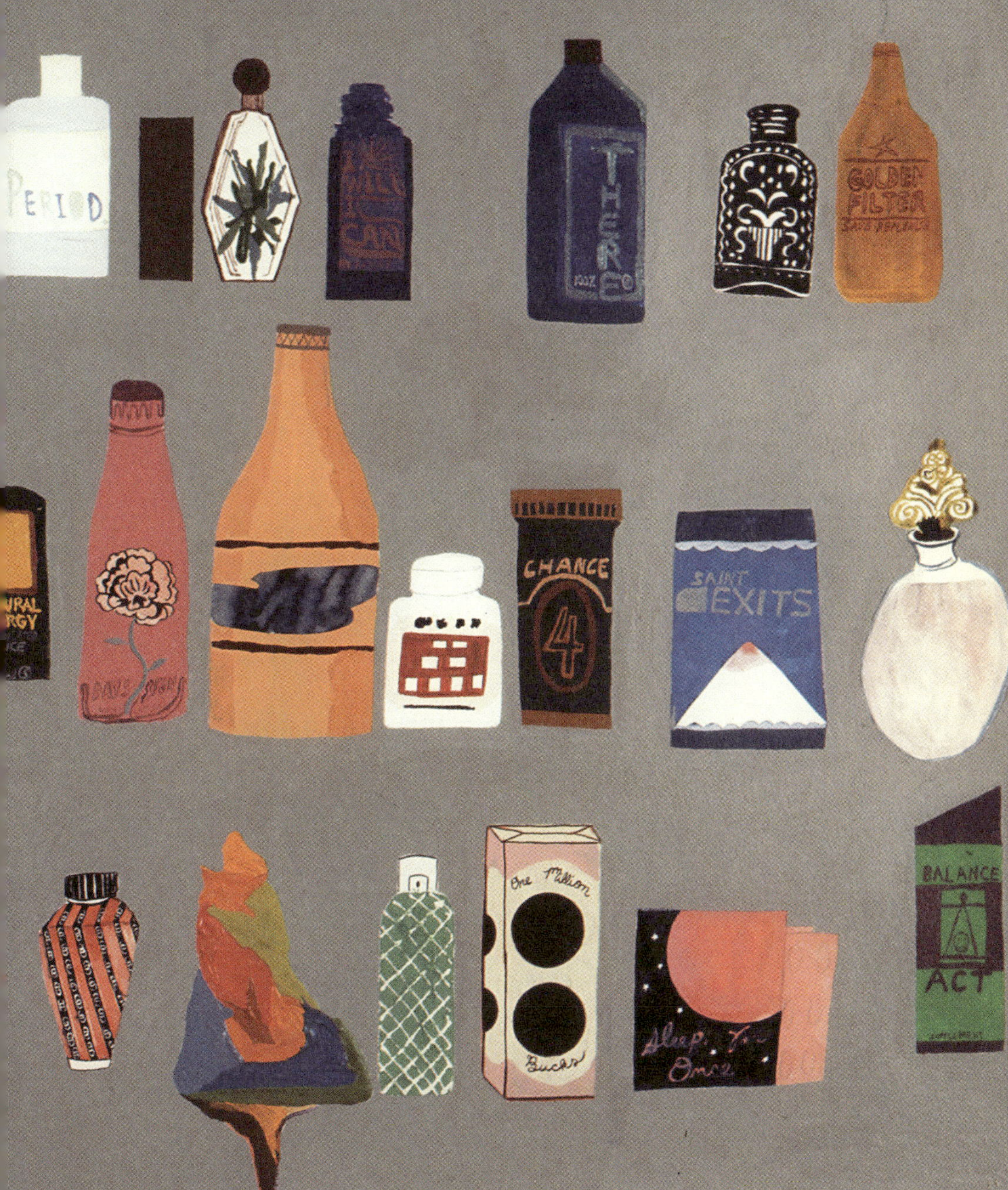

PERIOD.
AMERICAN CAN
THERE
GOLDEN FILTER
NATURAL ENERGY
CHANCE 4
SAINT EXITS
One Million Bucks
Sleep, You Once
BALANCE ACT

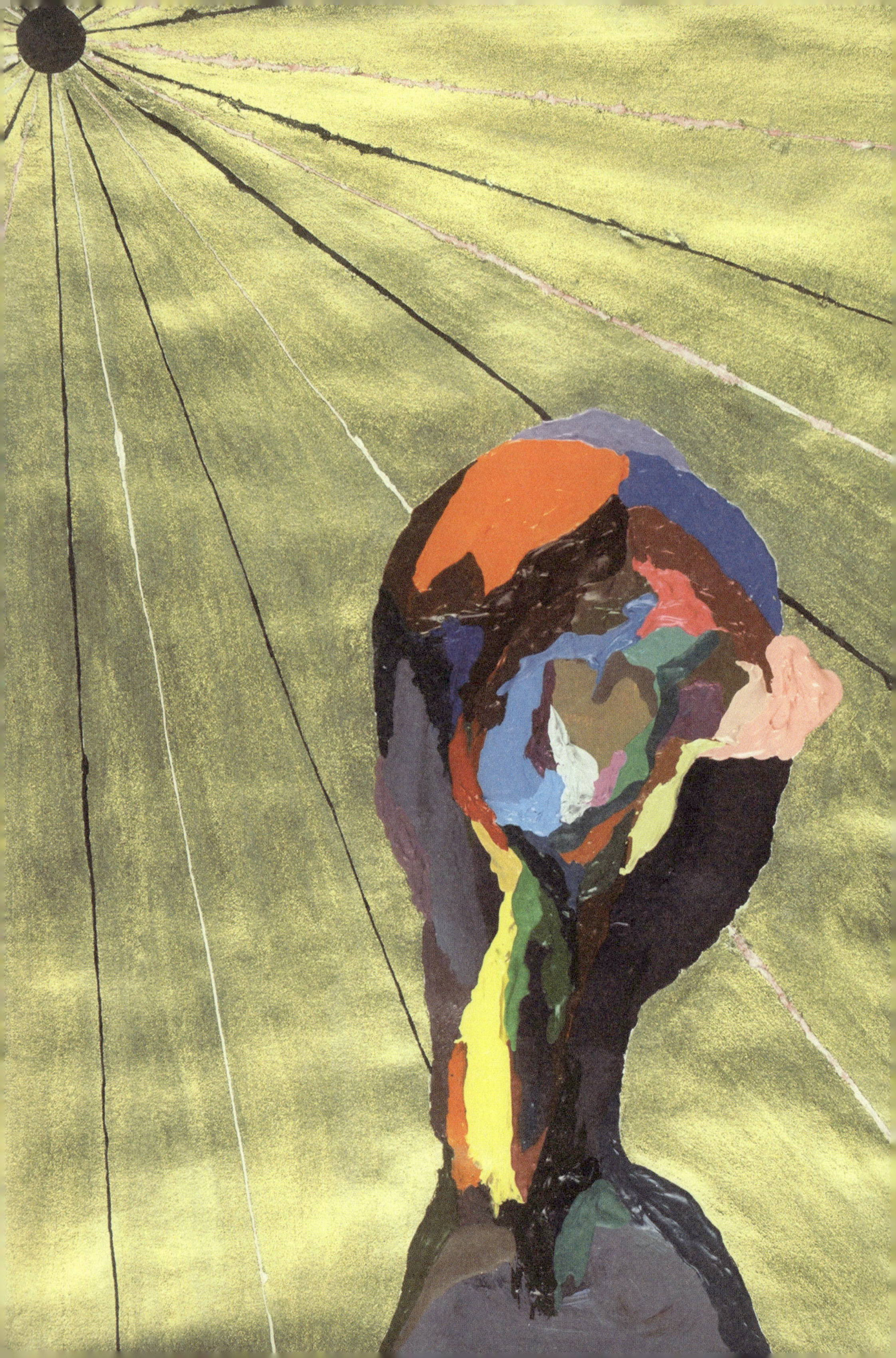